Everyday Materials

Paper

Andrew Langley

WAYLAND

First published in 2008
by Wayland

Copyright © Wayland 2008

Wayland
338 Euston Road
London NW1 3BH

Wayland Australia
Level 17/207 Kent Street
Sydney, NSW 2000

Editor: Annabel Savery
Designer: Ian Winton
Illustrator: Ian Winton
Picture researcher: Rachel Tisdale

Acknowledgements: Corbis: 12 (Sally A Morgan; Ecoscene). Discovery Picture Library:
1, 19 and 21 (Chris Fairclough). GettyImages: Cover (Garry Gay), 5 (Dorling Kindersley), 8
(Dr Dennis Kunkel). Istockphoto: cover and spread head panel, 4 (Carmen Martinez), 6
(Susan Trigg), 9 (Viktor Balabanov), 10 (Max Blain), 10 lower, 14 (Natalia Tkachenko), 15
(Rob Cruse), 16 (Yusuf Anil Akduyga), 17, 20 (Olga Shelego). M-Real: 13 and 18. Science
Photo Library: David R Frazier.

British Library Cataloguing in Publication Data
Langley, Andrew
    Paper. – (Everyday materials)
    1. Paper – Juvenile literature
    I. Title
    620.1'97

ISBN–13: 978 0 75025 319 2

Printed in China

Wayland is a division of Hachette Children's Books,
an Hachette Livre UK company.

Contents

What is paper?

There is paper everywhere. We read newspapers and books made of paper. We use paper napkins, bags and envelopes.

Paper can be used in many different ways. It is light and thin. It is also easy to bend and cut.

Eye spy

Look around your classroom. How many things are made of paper?

Different kinds of paper

There are thousands of different kinds of paper. Thinnest of all is **tissue paper**, which is very soft. Paper for books is thicker.

Eye spy

Find five kinds of cardboard in your home.

Brown wrapping paper is used for bags and **packaging**. **Cardboard** is thicker and stronger than paper. It is made of several layers of paper.

Cardboard is used to make boxes.

What is paper made of?

Paper is made of millions of tiny hairs.
These are called **fibres**.
They are tangled
together to
form a stiff
mat of
paper.

Look at this
close up of
paper fibres.

8

We can also make paper from straw.

Nearly all paper fibres come from wood. Other materials are also used, such as **cotton**, **linen** and **straw**.

What do you think?

It is easy to tear one sheet of newspaper. Now try tearing a whole newspaper. Why is it so difficult?

9

The pulp mill

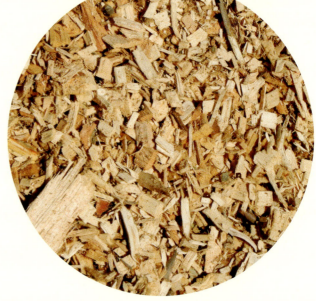

Logs of wood arrive at the **pulp mill**. A machine breaks them up into small chips. The chips are mixed with water and chemicals.

10

The mixture is heated in a big tank. The wood fibres become soft. The mixture turns into a mushy liquid called **pulp**.

Rolling and drying

The wet pulp comes out of the tank and is spread on **wire mesh**. Huge rollers squeeze the water out of the pulp. The water drains away through the holes in the wire mesh.

When the paper is dry it is rolled into huge rolls.

Eye spy

Can you find any paper on a roll in your home?

13

Creating paper

We can colour paper by adding **dyes** to the pulp. Paper for books is also **coated** with **size**. This is a glue which stops the ink from spreading over the paper.

Cups and cartons have a covering of wax or plastic. This stops liquid from soaking through the paper.

What do you think?

Which kind of paper soaks up water best – newspaper or shiny magazine paper?

15

Special uses

Folded inner layer

Corrugated board is even stronger than cardboard. It has three layers, like a sandwich. The middle layer of paper is shaped into folds.

We use paper in some surprising places. Car engines have paper **filters**. The filters keep the oil and air clean.

Did you know?

Paper was first made in China, nearly 2,000 years ago.

Paper is also used to make the face masks that surgeons wear.

Recycling paper

It takes a lot of wood to make paper. Most of this comes from new forests. The trees are planted to supply the pulp mills.

But old paper can be used again. The fibres in the paper can be turned to pulp and made into new paper.

Eye spy

Do you have a recycling bin at home? Do you put old newspapers into it?

Quiz

Questions

1. What is most paper made of?

2. What happens in a pulp mill?

3. How is the water squeezed out of the pulp?

4. What does bleach do?

5. What happens to wood fibres when they get wet?

Answers

5. Wood fibres go soft when they get wet.

4. Bleach takes the colour out of wood pulp.

3. Big rollers squeeze the water out of the pulp.

2. The wood is broken into chips and turned into pulp.

1. Most paper is made of wood.

20

Paper topic web

Geography
If you want to write to someone in another country you can buy special airmail paper. This paper is very light.

Art and design
You can make things with papier-mâché. This is mashed up paper mixed with glue. It can be moulded into shapes and decorated.

History
The first kind of paper was made by the Ancient Egyptians. It was made from a plant called papyrus.

Science
A type of paper called litmus paper changes colour in different liquids. Ask your science teacher to show you.

English
All the books you read are printed on paper. Read 'The Paper Bag Princess' by Robert Munsch. She has to wear a paper bag when a dragon burns all her clothes!

Glossary

bleach the chemical which removes the colour from materials

cardboard a strong kind of paper made from layers of pulp

coated covered with a thin layer of something

corrugated folded into a series of ridges or grooves

cotton cloth made from the fibres of the cotton plant

dye something which gives colour to a material

fibres the tiny, hair-like strands that make up trees and other plants

filter a very fine mesh, or something with small holes which stops dirt passing through it

linen cloth made from the fibres of the flax plant

packaging paper, card and other materials used to wrap up food and other products

pulp a mixture of wood fibres, water and chemicals

pulp mill a place where wood is mixed with water and turned into a soggy mixture called pulp

size a kind of glue used to coat paper

straw the stalks of wheat and other grain crops

tissue paper a fine, soft and thin kind of paper

wire mesh a flat net made of crossed metal wires

Further information

Books to read

Amazing Science: Materials. Sally Hewitt. Wayland, 2006.

Science Explorers: Paper: Exploring the Science of Everyday Materials.
   Nicola Edwards and Jane Harris. A & C Black Publishers, 2003.

Raintree Perspectives: Using Materials: How We Use Paper. Chris Oxlade.
   Raintree Publishers, 2004.

Start-Up Science: Materials. Claire Llewellyn. Evans Brothers Ltd, 2004.

Web sites to visit

BBC Schools
http://www.bbc.co.uk/schools/scienceclips/ages/5_6/sorting_using_mate.shtml
Learn all about different types of materials and their properties.

Confederation of Paper Industries Kids Korna
http://www.paper.org.uk/info/kids/homemade.htm
Learn how to make your own paper here.

Recycling guide
http://www.recycling-guide.org.uk/paper.html
Learn all about how paper is recycled.

Index

24